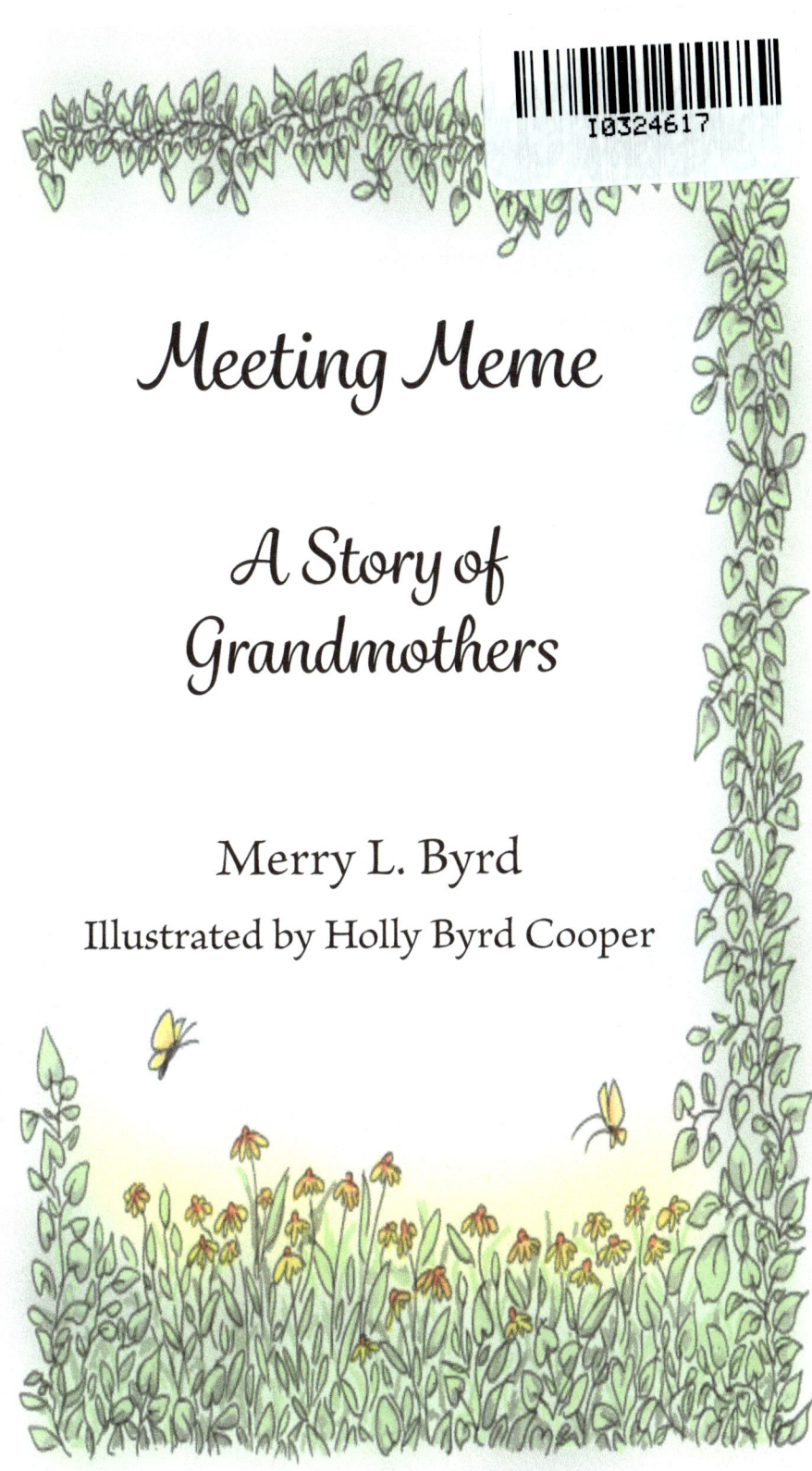

Meeting Meme

A Story of Grandmothers

Merry L. Byrd

Illustrated by Holly Byrd Cooper

Copyright © 2014 by Merry L. Byrd

All rights reserved.
No part of this book may be reproduced, transmitted, or stored in an information retrieval system in any form or by any means, graphic, electronic, or mechanical, including photocopying, taping, or recording, without prior written permission from the publisher. Scanning, uploading or distributing this book via the
Internet or via any other means without the permission of the publisher is illegal and punishable by law.

The book was typeset in Sanvito Pro and Grafolita Script.

Illustrations were created with ink, water color, and added digital enhancment.

Puffleg Press
www.puffleg.com

ISBN 978-0-9906389-1-9

For
Mayme Krause Hollingsworth,
1905 - 2004

When we were very young and you were taller,

you wore hats and hose and high-heeled shoes with just-peep-out toes.

We would watch you walk to church
and wonder
how you could walk
so tall and straight.

Sometimes we'd dress up too.

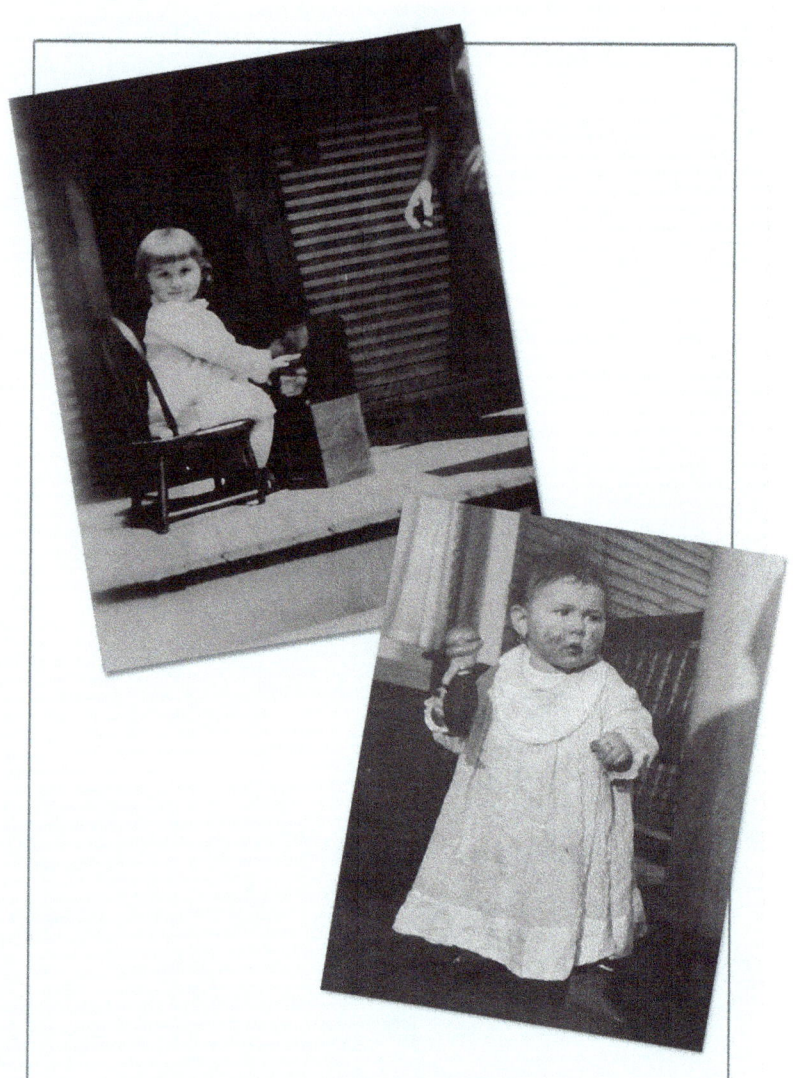

When we were very young
and you were taller,
we wanted to be just like you.

When we were very young and you were taller, you would fix oatmeal cookies almost every week and Angel Food cake with chocolate icing for our birthdays.

When we were
very young and you were
taller, you would let us daydream on
your sofa or play in your yard
whenever we were mad, in trouble
at home, sad, or
lonely.

At other times,
you sat on the floor with us and played
paper dolls, Uncle Wiggly, or Go Fish.

You would read us stories.

You would sleep with us when we were sick.

Once Holly had such terrible dreams that she
woke up and crawled into the top part of the
trundle bed to escape
the pink pig and the brown sailor bear.
They were chasing her in their boat
through the swamp.

You cuddled her close and said you would
always be there when she was scared.

Once we both were afraid to
go to the park because no one
would play with us.

You packed the
even-old-then-hamper
and walked us to the park
for a picnic.
You shared cherry tomatoes with
the girl who teased us and
helped us all become friends.

You said you would always walk with us
when we were afraid of where we were going.
You pushed us so high on the swing
that our toes touched the
oak tree's leaves.

Once, Merry was very sick and had
to see a doctor many miles away.

You sat in the back seat
with her while she sobbed
and pressed her hand to
calm the throbbing in her ear.

You went in to see the doctor with her,
still holding her hand tight.
You said, "I know this will be all right."
You let her see you right by her side,
as close as the fear, and as big.

Now we have grown a lot,
and you are some bit shorter
as we meet again to play.

Sometimes now your strong hands tremble,
and sometimes now you are afraid.
You cannot walk as quickly or surely
as you once did.
(And we two grandkids sometimes
still walk slow...)
But our best, best friend forever,
there are still places we can go.

You have showed us how to care
about people, plants, and things.
You have mopped and swept and dusted.
You once taped a broken wing.
You are so about the fixing.
You know so much of what you know.

You are also about helping --
mending dresses, toys, and such --
that we don't discuss the loving:
all the giving was to us.

Today you go to see the doctor because your eyesight has grown dim.

On one side, you just see grayness,
and it seems a cruel whim.
All the color is not gone though.

We just now must look within.

You dreamed last night that Edna
left you in the field four miles from home.
It was dark and slightly raining.
You felt very much alone.

Let us drive you to that pasture.
Take a picnic... Sit and wait...
For the night comes in
with moonlight,
and the flowers
stay awake.

Now that we are taller,
now that we are grown,
when you feel the dark or lonely,
we can share the love you've shown.

You can tell us where the fear is.
We will meet you at that place.
We can meet there where the fear is,
and our hearts can fill its space.

*So now that sometimes fear has found you,
let us take your hand and say:*

We can watch the sun set softly.
We can watch new children play.

www.ingramcontent.com/pod-product-compliance
Lightning Source LLC
Chambersburg PA
CBHW040555010526
44110CB00054B/2740